A TRUE BOOK™

Designing a Game

J E N N I F E R   H A C K E T T

Children's Press®
An Imprint of Scholastic Inc.

Content Consultant
Sarah Otts, Scratch Online Community Developer, MIT Media Lab

Library of Congress Cataloging-in-Publication Data
Names: Hackett, Jennifer, author.
Title: Designing a game / by Jennifer Hackett.
Description: New York, NY : Childrens Press, [2019] | Series: A true book | Includes bibliographical
    references and index.
Identifiers: LCCN 2018027254| ISBN 9780531127339 (library binding : alk. paper) | ISBN 9780531135426
    (pbk. : alk. paper)
Subjects: LCSH: Video games—Design—Juvenile literature. | Video games—Authorship—Juvenile
    literature.
Classification: LCC QA76.76.C672 H33 2019 | DDC 794.8/1525—dc23
LC record available at https://lccn.loc.gov/2018027254

Scholastic Inc., 557 Broadway, New York, NY 10012

1 2 3 4 5 6 7 8 9 10 R 28 27 26 25 24 23 22 21 20 19

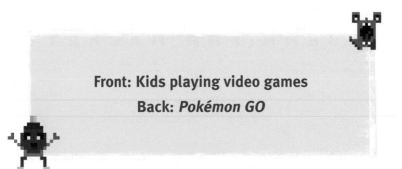

Front: Kids playing video games
Back: *Pokémon GO*

Find the Truth!

Everything you are about to read is true *except* for one of the sentences on this page.

Which one is **TRUE**?

T or F   The first video games were created in the 1990s.

T or F   Not every game has a way to win.

Find the answers in this book.

Contents

THE **BIG** TRUTH!

A New Way to Play

Virtual reality

Mario Tennis

This is Kelly. Help her on page 42!

About 65% of all U.S. homes have at least one device for playing video games.

Always ask permission from a parent or trusted adult before trying out a new video game.

CHAPTER 1

Game On

People around the world love playing all kinds of video games. Some people like platformers, where they control a character who jumps across platforms and avoids obstacles on the race to a finish line. Others enjoy strategy games that test their ability to solve challenges. From epic adventures to sports **simulations**, there are games that appeal to everyone. But where do these incredible games come from?

Playful Programs

Like the programs you use to surf the internet, watch videos, or do anything on a computer, video games are a type of **software**. All software is made up of instructions a computer follows to complete various tasks. Because computers do not understand the languages people use to communicate with each other, software is written using special programming languages. There are many different programming languages, and each has different uses.

Pokémon GO uses the GPS and camera systems on smartphones to make it look like Pokémon live in the real world.

Instructions written in programming languages are called code. Video games use code to tell a computer what to do as people play. Code determines how your character moves through the game world and how enemies behave. It tells the computer how to react when you press different buttons or use different strategies. In other words, it controls everything you can see and do in a game!

Developers plan out everything from levels to character designs when they are creating a new game.

Talented Teammates

A lot of work goes into making a video game. Even the simplest games can take countless hours of planning, coding, and testing to design. Some games are created by small, independent teams of **developers**. Others are built by hardworking individuals who handle every detail on their own. But the biggest blockbuster games require the efforts of dozens or even hundreds of developers.

Start Your Engines

Developers don't always code every detail of their games from scratch. Instead, they rely on a pre-built game **engine**. An engine is a collection of code for common game features. For example, it might contain code that can determine how characters move or how graphics are displayed. Developers can include this pre-built code in their games and modify it to suit their needs. This saves a lot of time and effort.

Developers often use motion capture technology to animate the characters in their games.

Sights and Sounds

A video game is more than just code. Graphics are the artwork you see on-screen as you play. Many modern games use detailed 3D graphics that can look almost like real life. Others stick to the traditional 2D style of older games. Both types of graphics are created by talented artists.

Sound effects and music are also important parts of most games. They can indicate when a player is doing well by playing triumphant music. Or they might create a feeling of danger with tense tunes.

Artists try to create characters that players will enjoy watching and identify with as they play a game.

The First Console

Long before the PlayStation 4 or the Nintendo Switch, there was the Magnavox Odyssey. Released in 1972, this device was the first home video game console. Between 1972 and 1975, more than 350,000 Odyssey consoles were sold. The Odyssey came with games already installed on it. They were mostly based on real-world sports such as tennis and hockey. The console also came with accessories such as dice and paper money. These were much like the pieces of a traditional board game. The Odyssey's graphics were very simple, made up mainly of dots on the screen. But that didn't stop people from having a ton of fun as they played!

The Magnavox Odyssey's physical game pieces helped people who were used to board games learn to enjoy video games.

GAME OVER

Modern video games have lifelike graphics that can make even sci-fi worlds seem realistic.

Game developers often create early artwork to show how they want the finished game to look.

CHAPTER 2

The First Steps

Have you ever played a really old video game? It was probably very simple, with blocky graphics and basic controls. Early games were limited by the low power of the computers that were available at the time. But today's games are usually far more complex. They can offer realistic 3D graphics and a nearly endless variety of gameplay styles. This means developers have a lot of decisions to make when they start planning a new game.

All Kinds of Games

The first thing developers need to consider is what type of gameplay their game will offer. For example, some games focus on avoiding obstacles. They rely on fast reflexes and quick thinking. Other games are all about exploration. Players go on adventures in a virtual world and search for hidden secrets. Games can also be based on strategic thinking, puzzle solving, or even telling an **interactive** story.

A game like *Tetris* requires strategic planning and fast reflexes.

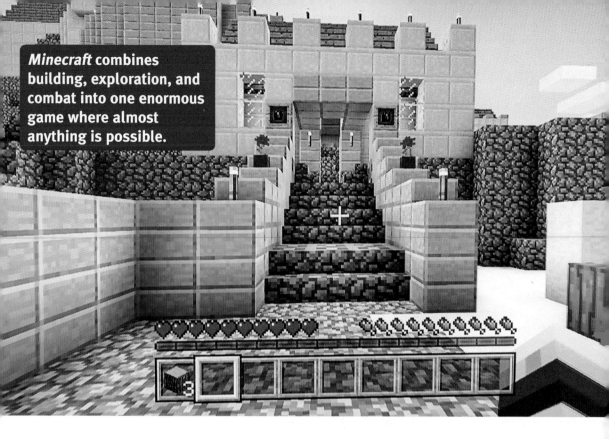

Minecraft combines building, exploration, and combat into one enormous game where almost anything is possible.

Many modern games combine several types of gameplay. For example, there are platforming games with exploration and puzzle elements. There are even games where you might switch between driving cars, fighting enemies, and playing sports. Sometimes a developer starts out with one simple idea, like a maze game, and then adds other types of gameplay to make it more interesting.

Some of the most famous characters from a huge variety of games come together in the popular *Super Smash Bros.* series.

Setting the Scene

Another thing developers consider when planning a game is whether or not it will have a story. Many modern games tell tales as exciting as your favorite TV shows or movies. Games that tell a story will need to have interesting characters. What will they look like? What are their goals? Developers also need to decide where the story will take place. Will it be set in a fantasy world or someplace real?

Keeping Score

All games need a goal for players to aim for. For example, some games simply require players to score points. The challenge comes from trying to beat your own high scores or outscore opponents.

Other games are based on completing tasks to move a story forward. Players win the game by getting to the end of the story. In some games, the goal is simply to play and be creative. There is no way to "win" and no score to keep track of!

In the hugely popular online game *Fortnite*, which is designed for kids ages 13 and up, players parachute onto a island and compete to be the last one standing in battles.

A New Way to Play

Virtual reality (VR) is an exciting new way to experience video games. By using special headsets and handheld controllers, players feel like they are really in the game world. They can use their whole body to interact with the game world. Players can move their heads around to look in different directions. They can control the game by moving their arms or walking around. Designing VR games presents many new challenges to game developers.

When wearing a VR headset, players can't see a controller or keyboard. This means the games need to be easy to play without relying on complex controls.

VR can be disorienting! Because what you see doesn't match up to what your body actually feels while playing VR, some players can get motion sickness. Developers need to take special steps to prevent this from happening. For example, they realized that one of the main things disorienting people was not being able to see their nose. As a result, many VR games now program in a fake nose for players to see!

In order to seem realistic, the graphics in VR games need to include a lot of small details that you wouldn't notice in a regular game. This can mean a lot of extra work for developers.

Students in China use VR to learn about nature in science class.

VR can help people experience things that might be difficult or impossible to do in real life.

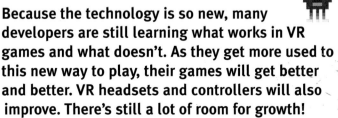
R equipment must e easy to control.

The Future of VR

Because the technology is so new, many developers are still learning what works in VR games and what doesn't. As they get more used to this new way to play, their games will get better and better. VR headsets and controllers will also improve. There's still a lot of room for growth!

With more than 100 million systems sold, the Nintendo Wii is one of the most popular game consoles ever.

Video games can be a great way to spend time with friends and family.

Deciding on Details

Video games are interactive. This means they let the player make choices that change things inside the game. This could be as simple as controlling the movement of a character on the screen. In a game with a story, the player's choices could change how that story ends. The player's actions decide whether the game ends or keeps going. A video game isn't just watched or read. It is experienced!

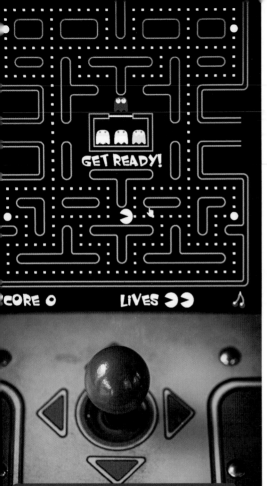

Games don't need to be complicated to be fun. In *Pac-Man*, tilting a joystick changes the direction of the game's main character. That is the only thing the player controls!

Controlling the Action

Once developers know what kind of game they want to make, it is time to start figuring out the details. One important thing is to decide how the game will be controlled. Will it use a keyboard, a controller, or a touch screen? What will each button do? A good game has **intuitive** controls. This means they are easy to understand even when the player isn't looking at his or her hands. A game should let you focus on the screen, not your controller!

Obstacles and Goals

Developers also need to decide which types of actions a player will be able to perform in the game. The game's setting, goals, and obstacles should match up with these actions. If there are enemies, the player must be able to defend or fight. If there are bottomless pits, the character needs to be able to jump.

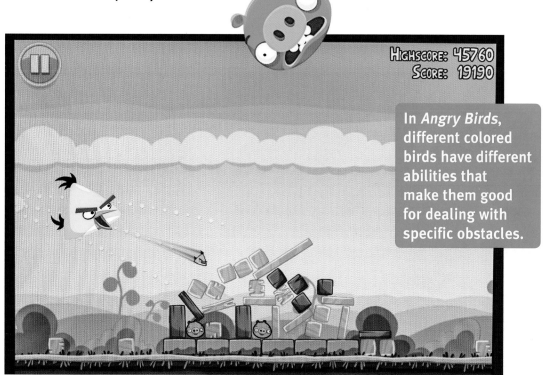

HIGHSCORE: 45760
SCORE: 19190

In *Angry Birds*, different colored birds have different abilities that make them good for dealing with specific obstacles.

Level Design

The way developers design levels and arrange obstacles has a big effect on how fun a game is. For example, imagine a game with a long section where all you do is run forward. Then you suddenly face many enemies at once. That doesn't sound very fun! Instead, the game should include a steady pace of challenges for the player. As levels go on, they can get more and more difficult.

In *Skylanders*, players can place action figures on a special platform to make different characters appear in the game.

In the *Splatoon* series, players must spray colorful ink onto walls to help them climb.

Hidden Secrets

Some of the best games use clever design to explain how the different levels should be played. The first levels are easier. They are designed to teach players how the game works. For example, a gap indicates a player needs to jump, while a ladder means a player needs to climb. Higher levels are trickier. They require players to think back to all the skills they have learned throughout the game.

Finding a Balance

A good game should not be too easy or too hard. It should provide a challenge, but it should not be so hard that it isn't fun anymore. It is tough to make a balanced game! If the spacing of jumps is slightly off, a level becomes frustratingly impossible. If a power-up is too strong, a level becomes too easy. If there are too many enemies, a game becomes impossible to survive.

Try thinking about a level as both a series of smaller parts and one long experience.

The Big Picture

When playing a game, you only see a bit of it at a time. But developers need to keep the entire game in mind as they work. Each level should be unique, but it should still feel like it is part of the same world as the other ones. Each level should also offer something new to keep players interested. This might be a new type of enemy, a greater challenge, or a story detail.

Programming languages such as Scratch and Blockly are designed especially for beginning coders.

CHAPTER 4

Putting the Pieces Together

By now, you might have a pretty good idea of what you want your own game to be like. As we learned earlier, all games are programmed using code. So how do you translate your design ideas into computer code? Becoming a coder means learning to think like a computer. Even though there are many programming languages, certain rules and techniques are a part of all of them.

It is never too early to start creating your own games.

Pressing Buttons

Part of a game's code involves recognizing **input** from a player. Players might use button presses to control a character's movement. Or they might use a joystick to change what part of the world the screen is showing. When a player presses a button, it completes a **circuit**. When the circuit is complete, it sends a signal to the computer. This signal triggers lines of code that tell the computer what to do next.

FROM THE CONTROLLER TO THE SCREEN

Pressing a button completes a circuit.

The circuit sends a signal to the computer.

Steps in Sequence

Computers understand things in a special way. They need sequences and **algorithms** to understand what they should do. A sequence is a set of instructions for the game to follow in a particular order. For example, when the game starts, a sequence might make a character go to the beginning of a maze, spin around once, and then say "let's go!"

The signal activates code.

The results show on the screen.

Amazing Algorithms

An algorithm is a specific kind of sequence that is used to solve a particular problem. For example, in a video game, algorithms turn the player's inputs into actions in the game. Some algorithms might take millions of steps to make the game character react after a button is pressed. Algorithms are often represented by flowcharts.

Timeline of Video Game History

1958
William Higinbotham creates *Tennis for Two*, the first video game.

1964
The programming language BASIC is created, making games much easier to program.

1972
The first home game console, the Magnavox Odyssey, is released.

1989
The Nintendo Game Boy is released, popularizing handheld video games.

1958 · 1964 · 1972 · 1989

If, Then

Video game code often relies on conditional statements. These statements say that if a certain thing happens, then another thing must happen. In a maze game, a conditional statement might say, "If a player steps on a certain square, then an obstacle will appear." Many different conditional statements layered together make an exciting game where new obstacles appear all the time!

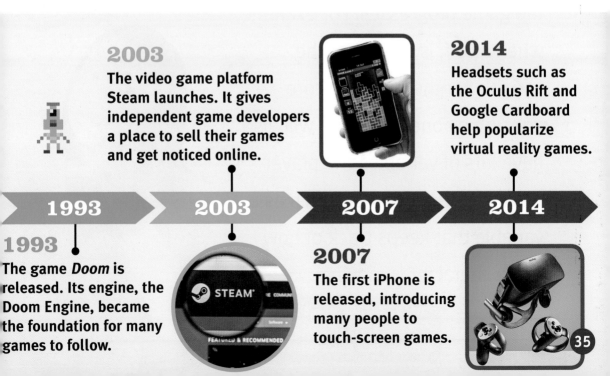

2003
The video game platform Steam launches. It gives independent game developers a place to sell their games and get noticed online.

2014
Headsets such as the Oculus Rift and Google Cardboard help popularize virtual reality games.

| 1993 | 2003 | 2007 | 2014 |

1993
The game *Doom* is released. Its engine, the Doom Engine, became the foundation for many games to follow.

2007
The first iPhone is released, introducing many people to touch-screen games.

Dealing With Variables

As you play a game, there are many changing numbers that the game must keep track of. For example, it needs to track how much time has passed. The number of health bars a character has left also might need to be recorded. Games use an element of code called a variable to keep track of any number that can go up or down. A variable can store and change information as the game progresses. For example, when a coin is collected, the variable for the player's score goes up by one. The code will also have lots of variables the player can't see on the screen, such as a variable that keeps track of how fast a character is moving.

Keeping track of a bunch of variables at once is very hard for a human, but easy for a computer.

Balls that fall from random locations along the top of the screen will be harder for players to catch than ones that fall from the same places.

Realistically Random

Developers need to keep their games exciting. One of the ways they do this is by using randomness. Imagine a game where you have to catch objects that fall from the top of the screen. It would be boring if every object fell from the same spot. Randomness is often created in code by using a random number generator. Each possible location the object might fall from is assigned a number value. The code randomly selects a number. Whatever location is associated with that number is where the object will fall from.

Starting Small

Making a game can seem like an overwhelming task. But many developers start small and work their way up to complicated games. Over time, they layer many parts together to create something truly impressive. If you want to code a game, try starting small!

- Create a character and a goal for the character to achieve. Think of three obstacles that will stand in its way.

- Write a sequence that tells how to play a classic game, like tennis or Simon Says. Consider what other directions a computer would need to re-create it.

- Try making a game with Scratch, a programming language designed especially for kids. 🚀

Misbehaving Code

Sometimes things go wrong when testing code. Small errors in the code can make a game unplayable! To prevent this, game developers **debug** their code. To help in the debugging process, developers often ask very attentive players to play their games, looking for errors or parts where the code doesn't work as it should. These players are called quality assurance testers. Once they spot an error, the developers need to figure out how to fix it. Sometimes the fix is as simple as correcting a spelling mistake. Other times, entire sections of code need to be rewritten!

Debugging gets its name from Grace Hopper, a computer scientist in the U.S. Navy. She spotted moths in a computer that had stopped running. The original computer bugs were actual bugs!

Debugging a game requires a lot of hard work and creative thinking.

Grid Guides

To keep track of the relationship between characters within a game's world, game designers use coordinate planes. Coordinate planes break levels and areas within the game into neat grids.

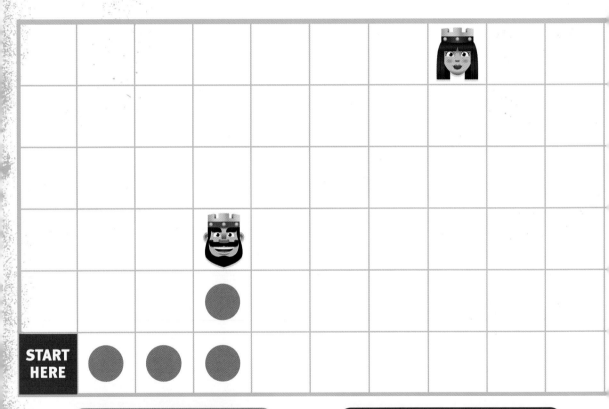

1. How many spaces right would you need to move to reach Character 1? How many spaces up?

2. From Character 1, you want to visit Character 4. How many spaces over and up would you need to move?

To reach other characters, treasure chests, doors, and more, the player character moves along this grid until it reaches a point of interest. Determine where each character is on the coordinate plane. Then move your player character to each spot!

KEY

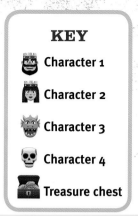

Character 1

Character 2

Character 3

Character 4

Treasure chest

3. From Character 4, you want to talk to Character 2. How many spaces over and up would you need to move?

4. From Character 2, you want to reach the treasure chest and then move to Character 3. How many spaces would you need to move and in which directions?

Answers: 1. 3, 2; 2. 16; 3. 4, 13; 4. 13 right, 4 down, 8 left

41

Creative Coding

Code is made up of different commands. A very simple kind of code gives instructions that can be followed. When designing games, developers test their code to make sure it works correctly. Check out these scenarios and choose the correct code to make the game do what it is supposed to.

SCENARIO 1

Which code will take the princess to the treasure chest without running into the dragons guarding it?

a. Move 4 right and 5 down

b. Move 4 down, 3 right, 1 down, and 1 right

c. Move 2 left, 5 down, and 5 right

d. Move 5 down and 4 right

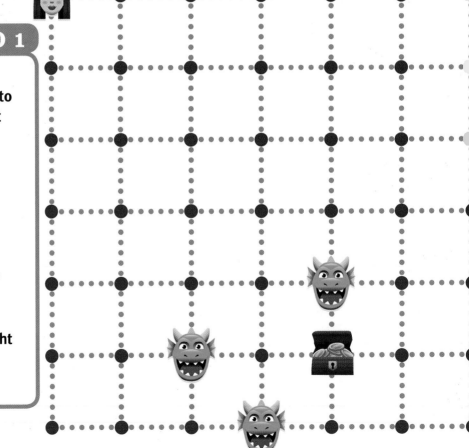